Find Your Passion

Live the Way You Want and Discover Your Purpose

Book 1 of the Quality Life Series

I0505432

Logan Hawkins

Contents

What is Passion?

P assion is not obvious, like the ability to throw a football, being a gifted musician or a talented craftsman, or living as an amazing inventor. Passion is not on a conscious level, something that you are thinking about daily and noticing. Passion is more "energetic" in nature and therefore, hard to see.

People say they are passionate about their kids, families, hobbies, etc. While these are all admirable, I would say these are interests that bring joy and pleasure. They may also be the tip of your passion or an indicator of your passion. While passion is a common word to describe an emotional state of liking something a lot, the passion we are talking about here is a much bigger concept. Here, it is about the core attributes that drive you and get you excited about life and living.

It is also important to recognize people often confuse passion with purpose. As I see it, purpose is the vehicle you ride because of your passion: your purpose is what you do (ex. playing sports, writing music, reading literature, or parenting.). Passion is the fuel and energy you use to drive: passion is how you are fueled (ex. by creativity, by problem-solving, or by helping people).

Passion is the internal fire burning inside you as a result of using your natural gifts, talents, and purpose here on Earth. You have passion before you use it, but it is like a match unlit. Passion gets lit when you use your gifts, talents, and purpose and results in personal fulfillment and "life in the flow," where everything works together and every area of your life is filled with joy, contentment, and synergy.

Why have passion? Is it possible everyone has a passion or are some people just more "emotional?"

Passion is seen as you look out into the world and selflessly allow yourself to be an instrument, using your gifts and talents. As you do this, you will begin to see your reflection and therefore, can more readily identify your passion. After you identify your passion, by experiencing the lit fire inside, you are able to focus on and use those gifts and talents more, and then your purpose and passion are united and drive the most fulfilling adventure of your life!

The reward of living a life of passion is incredible! Once you have tasted it, you will crave for its return. It is an amazing overflowing of your heart, body, mind, and soul. You have energy, direction, purpose, and focus. As humans, we all want this, but sometimes it seems too hard to achieve, so we give up, and decide to just enjoy what life gives us.

"What life gives us?" I ask. Don't be fooled, we are not here on Earth to be floating down a river on an inner tube, just passively taking in what life has to offer. You will not find passion in that inner tube. You might hit some rapids and get a little taste of it here and there, however, if you want to know what living a life of passion means and is, you have to go look for it.

Life can dish out some hard knocks, tough lessons, challenges, and adversity. How you handle those are up to you. You see, there is a quote that states, "Life is 10% what happens to you and 90% what you do with it." The more you can look at life as a lesson, something to learn from and a gift, the happier you will be. The more you are living in your purpose and passion, the easier it is to see things from this perspective. Do you want to have this synergy in your heart, body, mind, and soul? Do you want to be content, overflowing with joy and being of value to the world?

Passion is your fuel. It motivates you to press on. It propels you up the mountain of your dreams and goals. If you have a passion for life, for people, for animals, for your causes and your convictions, and you will be nearly unstoppable. You should be a champion for those who have great needs and can't do anything about it themselves. Speak with passion, teach with passion, lead with passion, love with passion, play with passion, and enjoy with passion.

Someone who is passionate is intriguing to watch and to listen to. They are usually energizing to be around.

They put great care into each and every detail of what they have a passion for. A passionate musician plays a piece over and over until it is perfection for her and the audience. Each sound is perfectly crafted and resonates purely, hauntingly, and brilliantly. Every song on the album may not be perfect, and sometimes it misses the mark, but we recognize the passion and are moved by the story told, how it was done and perhaps why it was done.

Passion draws people in, and to you. They want to be part of that passion. They want to be as motivated as you are. They want to touch that passion, and embrace it. Passion lifts people up to a new level, which they can feel for themselves and from you. Passion encourages and whips new energy into people and projects. Everyone wants to feel passion for something.

When you come to roadblocks in life, your passion is what brings you beyond each and every halt. When there is passion involved, you have a need to move forward, and reach beyond every expectation towards the fulfillment of your dreams and goals. If you get stopped in life, and if you have passion for life or for an aspect of your work, dig deep within yourself to find what really motivates and captivates you, and then find brand-new aspects of your passion or your love you have not seen before. You find new doors to open; you gravitate towards other passionate people. You create new paths with your passion and deep desires.

A person who does not have that passion can wallow in the low points of her life, and have great trouble finding the meaning of it. You must give meaning to your own life. You must discover the passions of your life and work. Most times, passions in your life develop slowly. You start by doing things you enjoy doing: cooking, painting, photography, performing, etc. When you find a certain thing you really enjoy, spend more time doing it. Learn about it, develop your interest and your knack for it, and find ways to become more involved with your hobby or pastime. When you start to become passionate about something, then you want to spend as much of your time as you can by being in and around it.

You want to learn everything you can about it. You want to be with other people who have your same interests and passions. Their passion and love fuels your passion.

Remember, small things can become big dreams if you are passionate about them. Take care of the small details with the same care and regard as if it were a great big event and you will move up the mountain with a steady sure foot.

Passionate leaders recognize passionate people, and the details of passion, and they hire and promote passionate workers, and create openings for those people. You can be passionate about anything. And remember that anything becomes something to the right person. Small or large, if you are passionate about it, you can see huge results; your passion can take you to great places.

You can make your living by doing what you love to do, if someone wants to pay you for what you love to do. If you can't find a boss who loves what you do, you can be your own boss. Start your own company if you are passionate enough about what you are doing. Either way, your passion will open a new door. Other people will become aware of your passion and your services. There are many customers out there for your services; you just have to find, target, and market to them.

That is not always easy, and sometimes it is very difficult when you are creating a new niche market. But if you can sustain yourself and grow and develop your client base, you will create the flow you want and need, to lead the life you desire for yourself.

Many times you cannot do it on your own, and that is when your passion will lead you to a partner or a team with your same passion that can help you. Now you can do it together as a team that is as passionate for your goals as you are. You and they become stronger as you work together.

Your goals may change a little bit, but the same underlying passion is still there and is being fed every day by your team. What you thought was impossible on your own has now become a possibility and you are rewarded for it. Your life, and their lives, begin to be satisfying.

It is thrilling when you begin to watch your dreams become realities, and you can all share in the victory together. Now the team has developed a reputation of excellence and passion. You will see that more creative and energetic people are drawn to the team because they like what they are seeing.

Because of that, your team will be able to do more than they could before, and do more awesome projects. Your team will be able to scale impossible heights in a very short period of time, and perhaps you will reach the greatest pinnacles of success you have ever dreamed about.

So have passion, take risks, step out in faith. Live a passionate life, and you will attract other passionate people, and you will fulfill your dreams. Tell yourself "I embrace the fullness of my life." Do it. You won't regret a minute of your life that way.

The Power of Passion

There once was a man, Jack, who worked very hard in his job. He had gone to school in an area of interest and got a job working in a like industry. He found a good wife and they had 3 wonderful children. Life was good in his adult years, but he found himself feeling like he was just on the treadmill of life. He got up every morning, he went to a job that he liked but where he longed for a break, some type of long-awaited vacation.

He had lost most of his hobbies, due to the time restraints of working many hours at his job, balanced with trying to take care of and spend time with his family. The dreams Jack had talked about in his youth (travel, starting his own business, becoming an amateur golf player, winning fantasy football, etc.) were still in the back of his mind, but only faintly.

Jack had a successful life by American standards (income, job, home, family, etc.), but he did not jump out of bed in the morning: he did not have a spring in his step and he seemed to carry a high level of stress. In general, he was happy, but not HAPPY.

This is a story of a man with a great life, but of a man who is lacking PASSION.

What is passion?

Webster defines passion as "a strong liking or desire for or devotion to some activity, object, or concept."

I define passion as an internal subconscious emotional calling that fuels the perspective, focus and actions you take as you live life and fulfill your purpose in life.

Passion is not obvious, like the ability to throw a football, being a gifted musician or a talented craftsman, or living as an amazing inventor. Passion is not on a conscious level, something that you think about daily and notice. Passion is more "energetic" in nature and therefore hard to see.

People say they are passionate about their kids, families, hobbies, etc. While these are all admirable, I would say these are interests that bring joy and pleasure. They may also be the tip of your passion or an indicator of your passion. While passion is a common word to describe an emotional state of liking something a lot, the passion we are talking about here is a much bigger concept. Here, it is about the core attributes that drive you and get you excited about life and living.

It is also important to recognize people often confuse passion with purpose. As I see it, purpose is the vehicle you ride because of your passion: your purpose is what you do (ex. playing sports, writing music, reading literature, or parenting.). Passion is the fuel and energy you use to drive: passion is how you are fueled (ex. by creativity, by problem-solving, or by helping people).

Passion is the internal fire burning inside you as a result of using your natural gifts, talents, and purpose here on Earth. You have passion before you use it, but it is like a match unlit. Passion gets lit when you use your gifts, talents, and purpose and results in personal fulfillment and "life in the flow," where everything works together and every area of your life is filled with joy, contentment, and synergy.

Why have passion? Is it possible everyone has a passion or are some people just more "emotional?"

Passion is seen as you look out into the world and selflessly allow yourself to be an instrument, using your gifts and talents. As you do this, you will begin to see your reflection and therefore, can more readily identify your passion. After you identify your passion, by experiencing the lit fire inside, you can focus on and use those gifts and talents more - your purpose and passion are united and drive the most fulfilling adventure of your life!

The reward of living a life of passion is incredible! Once you have tasted it, you will crave for its return. It is an amazing overflowing of your heart, body, mind, and soul. You have energy, direction, purpose, and focus. As humans, we all want this, but sometimes it seems too hard to achieve, so we give up, and decide to just enjoy what life gives us.

"What life gives us?" I ask. Don't be fooled, we are not here on Earth to be floating down a river on an inner tube, just passively taking in what life has to offer. You will not find passion in that inner tube. You might hit some rapids and get a little taste of it here and there, however, if you want to know what living a life of passion means and is, you have to go look for it.

Life can dish out some hard knocks, tough lessons, challenges, and adversity. How you handle those are up to you. You see, there is a quote that states, "Life is 10% what happens to you and 90% what you do with it." The more you can look at life as a lesson, something to learn from and a gift, the happier you will be. The more you are living in your purpose and passion, the easier it is to see things from this perspective. Do you want to have this synergy in your heart, body, mind, and soul? Do you want to be content, overflowing with joy and being of value to the world?

Jack Finds Passion

Jack got tired of stumbling through life. He did some investigation and found out a few things: he enjoys the outdoors, being invigorated by the fresh air, strategic thinking, and intellection. Earlier, when he was playing golf he was engaging in a few of these passions, an appreciation of nature, strategic thinking, and intellection. He had stopped playing golf because of a lack of time. The irony is that after picking the hobby back up, he now seems to have more time and energy.

At work, he also noticed his job had become dull because he was not reading the statistical reports like he had when he first started his job. Back then, when he read the reports, it motivated him and got him excited about driving strategies that would save the company time and money. So, he started reading the reports again and found himself more engaged at work. The momentum helped him do things faster, be more positive and actually finish up on time many days so he could get home to his kids.

Since Jack was getting home on time, there was a little break before dinner when he could go outside and play with the kids. He loved throwing the ball and teaching little Jake how to ride his bike! It even inspired him to equip the family to embrace Saturday morning walks on the local park trail.

As Jack realized his passions were being outside in nature, using his intellectual abilities and creating solutions and strategies. He found that these same things showed up in every area of life. It was exciting and compelling! He was happy, fulfilled and had found a synergy in every area of his life.

You now know what passion is. You now know the benefit of inviting passion into your life. Take the time to explore your personal passions and to integrate them into your life. Passion is a phenomenal gift. If you want to LIVE life to the fullest and enjoy it along the way, take the time to discover your passions. Put them into your daily life. You will find you have time for everything you did before and more.

How to Live Your Passion

I work with people every day who are eager to improve themselves, but I don't think that's always the direct path to someone's ultimate happiness. I think the fastest, most direct way to achieve anything in life it to identify, follow, and ultimately LIVE your passion.

Passion can carry different connotations for different individuals. We can make it simple enough. Your passion is that thing that makes your day worth living. No matter what happens, you find at least a few minutes to think about, focus on and do that one thing you are passionate about. The problem with most people is when they think about their passion while not LIVING their passion, they are in a place of lack and scarcity around their passion.

In other words, they are frustrated and unhappy because they think they have to do without the one thing they are passionate about. This kind of thinking can wreak havoc on your soul and create a terrible direction for your future self to follow. So let's take a few steps to get back on track using the above example of a person looking to improve their fitness and more specifically, their body composition.

Identify Your Passion

Chances are if they are in my office asking for help, they aren't passionate about exercise and fitness. I have a few athletes who come through my office, but the majority of them are just looking to get back on track and shed a few pounds. Therefore, we need to find the passion. We can use fitness to help that person live for their passion, that's the easy part. If this person was truly passionate about life, no part of their experience would be negative. This includes the physical body.

If this person can identify their passion and define what makes them ultimately happy, then fitness, nutrition, and everything else will play a supporting role in helping that person live their passion. It truly doesn't matter what the passion is. The main goal for step one is identifying it. You don't have to pry too hard... they will be more than excited to tell you all about it!

Follow Your Passion

This is the step most people get tripped up on. Your passion drives you. It either drives your success or drives you crazy thinking about it! Once you identify your passion and make it crystal clear in your mind, it will keep coming up. It will give you nudges. Some will be subtle and some will very obvious. Your only role in achieving your ultimate goals is to take action on these nudges.

Some call this inspired action. I think that's the perfect way to describe it. If it feels like too much work, the inspiration isn't there and your energy is best spent elsewhere. But when your passion comes up, pay attention to it. Once you take a few small steps toward your passion, the path will unfold before you and more and more opportunities will come up.

For each new nudge that is given to you, you must give thanks for it. This will assure you continue to get them! As a disclaimer, drastic and very large action is fine if it is inspired. However, there's no reason to quit your job and rush out to chase your dreams. In most cases, leaving the security of a job or relationship creates stress and fear and can stop the flow inspired thoughts coming to you. Take small, but constant action towards your passion. There is great joy in this process.

Living Your Passion

The third and final step is all anyone ever wants. It's living your passion. While living your passion, you are happy. You are in a loving and accepting place. You let things come to you and love your life. Since you are in are giving off such great energy, those around you enjoy your company. In fact, the happier you are with your passion, the more you share it in many forms! It truly is a great place and one everyone should experience.

This by no means implies there will not be negative situations that arise. Make sure they do not distract you from your passion. It is what you are living for. What you are meant to do. It is what God, the universe, The Divine, or whatever you chose to address it as, wants for you. In fact, it was yours all along, and that's why you have always have a strong desire to chase it!

To sum it up, we can find happiness in chasing and living our passion. But the absolute truth is the process works in completely the opposite order. The happier you are NOW, the more opportunities you have to live your passion. Let's finish with our hypothetical client from earlier (you thought I forgot didn't you!)

Let's say this person's ultimate goal is to attract a mate. This is why that person is seeking advice on fitness and weight loss. Therefore, their level of deservingness is tied to their physical appearance and they believe by changing that one variable, they will become confident and attract the mate of their dreams. Their passion may be to settle down with the perfect mate, have a family and enjoy all the wonderful feelings of love and growing old with someone. What a great feeling!

So if you get down to the passion, none of that has anything to do with fitness or exercise! However, by taking small steps towards achieving personal goals in fitness this personal can start to build confidence and therefore deem themselves worthy of such a life! In this scenario, the person will use fitness and exercise to build confidence and clarity in regards to their passion. Each trip to the gym, or pound of body fat lost creates a chain reaction of passionately inspired action which leads them to a life of passion.

Solving the Puzzle

We all are looking to solve the "passion puzzle" within ourselves, but how exactly can you learn how to find your passion?

Well, for starters, if you're reading this, you're probably off to the wrong start. Does that surprise you?

It was meant to.

Because, as someone who truly wants you to find your passion, you must be advised right here that it can't be found by simply reading (although it's a good beginning).

The passion puzzle is solved by doing... if you're not doing, you're not learning how to find your passion...

Here's the thing: The answer to how to find your passion lies in your heart, not your head.

Therefore, unless you decide here and how to take action in doing something to find your passion, you're likely to just continue going about your activities of daily living like a robot, just going through the actions of life and never feeling fulfilled...

Sound familiar?

That's because most of us are caught up in the "life trap," which is really not a trap at all. But fear of change keeps us trapped where we are, and our perception of our life is just hum-drum and boring.

Truth be told, animals are better at knowing their purpose than humans, because they follow "instincts," which is another way of what we intellectuals call "listening to God." A bear in the woods knows his passion because he's living daily in the present, and hunting for whatever life brings him, continually staying sensitive to the signs around him.

But take that same bear and put a cage around him for a year. After he gets over angrily growling at everything passing by, he eventually realizes he might as well just stay calm and wait for the food that's being brought to him.

Ironically, should we decide to let him out a year later, will he decide to go back to his exciting and purpose driven life in the woods? No! He actually won't venture out any further than the boundaries of his cage.

We as humans have to guard against making our lives "too comfortable." Because it's only when we are willing to get out of our comfort zone a little bit that we can grow. And it's in doing and growing that we actually develop our purpose and find our passion.

To get you started, here's a beginning exercise to learn how to find your passion.

Get a piece of paper or type on your Word doc, "What is my passion?"

Then type an answer - just the first thing that comes to your mind. Keep asking yourself questions and answering them, like in this example:

What is my passion? I want to help people.

How? I want to help people achieve success in their life

What kind of success?

I want to help people to get in touch with their inner self and discover how to be happy.

Keep doing the above exercise until you find an "answer" that makes you cry.

This could take 20 minutes, or it could take hours, day, or weeks. The final answer you tell yourself is your answer from your "inner self," and you are beginning to reach your inner soul.

But learning how to find your passion is only the beginning...

You must work to develop your passion by continually stretching. By this I mean get out of your comfort zone and do something that scares you just a little. Now, I'm not talking about doing something you know you absolutely hate!

Finding your passion is about finding what you love - what you were meant for. And this is the reason for completing step one before you go on with this formula.

The next step will stretch you a little further... find your passion by blogging...

When you spend a little time each day expressing yourself in a personal way on "paper" (or online on your computer), each post will bring you to a higher level of skill, and closer to your Inner Self and your true purpose.

When you start blogging, you're likely to learn more about yourself...

What do you love to talk about, learn, or teach others?

And, once you start getting comments from your readers, pay attention to how it makes you feel. That feeling is your key to your true passion.

All you need to do is tap into your feelings as you're constructing your blog posts, and you'll become more and more aware of how to find your passion. I'm passionate about sharing this with you!

And why is it so important to learn how to find your passion?

Because once you discover your passion, you won't give up. You will have the drive and energy to enjoy what you're doing.

I once heard that the secret to becoming a millionaire is to find something you love that will make you money.

And, with Internet marketing (or actually achieving any success in life), persistence is golden.

Step three to how to find your passion is simple: Quit talking and start doing!

"The way to get started is to quit talking and begin doing."

-Walt Disney: American film producer, director, animator, entrepreneur, and philanthropist

You can't steer a ship that's not moving. Likewise, you will never be able to grow to find your true passion unless you start doing! This is YOUR LIFE I'm talking about.

Don't wait until you "have everything perfect." You never will.

7 Tips for Living a Purposeful Life

As three-part beings, humans have a mind, the body and the soul, and passion is the soul seeking self-realization and actualization. The root emotion of passion is love, therefore passionate living is daily experiences that move into and towards love.

Simply put, a passionate life is a life whereby you are acting out the urge to experience your true self, experiencing passion in your physical reality.

When living on purpose and passionately, you will find yourself to be more inspired and more energized, daily. Who doesn't want more inspiration and energy in their life? Have you ever been in the presence of someone who was so ridiculously happy and fired up about what they did in their life?

The power of passion is magnetic to say the least, and the following 7 tips are ways that will help YOU get that much closer to living a passionate life of your own:

Use Your Imagination and get Creative

It is very natural to conjure up ideas about all sorts of things, all day long. And all day long, your mind systematically processes on average 70,000 thoughts per day. I invite you to consider using one of those thoughts as an opportunity to think about what passionate living means to you?

Maybe it means flying jet planes in Thailand, or running multiple businesses worldwide. Maybe it means helping the orphans in Africa, or working with researchers in the Cure Cancer societies. Or maybe it means spending every weekend with your best friends and family. Remember when you were younger? And the ideas seemed to run rampant? Remember when you were free?

Well, the truth is, you are still just as free now as you were then, but the way you thought about things changed. Being creative is a natural gift everyone possesses, it is just a matter of tapping back into the intuitive creativity. Use your imagination!

Actively Remove the "Dream Squashers" in Your Life

All passionate people surround themselves with other passionate, uplifting people. They choose to hang out with people who either support or facilitate their very being, and act as a complimentary addition to their lives. A "Dream Squasher" is someone who has nothing better to do but rain on everyone's parade. They are quick to judge, quick to say no, and quick to take advantage. Exactly the kind of people who ruin the very thought you may have of pursuing your passion, and creating your dreams. Even if you try, it is human nature to assimilate the environment you are in, so a powerful tip to living your passionate life is to actively remove the "Dream Squashers."

Make The Things You Love An Official Priority

Take a moment right now to list your top three (3), all-time favorite things to do. Write them down in less than a minute. I challenge you to do this right now. The first 3 things to came to your mind upon answering to this challenge are very likely a genuine list of the things you love to do. With these 3 activities in mind, purposefully schedule in these activities as often as you can in your calendar (Google Calendar, your agenda, your iPhone or Blackberry, etc) right now. Amazingly, people tend to do the things they write down, and tend to forget about the things that are just passing thoughts. Successful and passionate people not only choose to do the things they love, they actually schedule it in. Make it an official priority!

Avoid Things that Make You Say, "Yuck!"

Have you ever been around someone you absolutely felt "turned off" by? Have you ever participated in an activity and just felt completely repulsed by it? Have you ever said yes to something, when you deep down you just wanted to say no? All of these emotional and psychological triggers have significance in deciding where to spend your time. Passionate people choose wisely, and say yes to the things that feel good, and feel right for them. If it makes you say (think or feel) "Yuck!" then start making the daily habit of avoiding these things all together.

Get A Coach

All passionate and purposeful people have ways to track and measure their personal success. Success just means you have achieved objectives or goals that you made in advance. You decide what success means to you, and in this case, the successful state is actually living more passionately and literally being in love with your life. Successful people also ensure they keep themselves accountable to what they say they will do.

All talk and no action make for a very phony life, so it is always wise to get a coach. If you have the available funds to invest in yourself, there are many professionals available and ready to come to your aid. If you don't have the funds immediately, there are always cost-effective options such as "hiring" a very reliable friend who is already doing some of the things you wish to accomplish. A qualified amateur would be someone who is at least doing all of the things you want to do successfully and consistently. Stay accountable to your desire of living passionately and get a coach.

Lighten Up

All passionate people only focus on that which brings them joy and brings them closer to their truest, most authentic selves. So having too much on their plate (literally and figuratively) is not an option in living life to the fullest. We hear the old adage, "Less is More" and as most experts will tell you, there is much truth to this statement.

Is there something you can let go of, that is simply wasting your time and energy? Do you also have some body issues whereby you are holding on too much excess weight? Now is the time to actively participate in removing the things in your life, and in your body, that are weighing you down. This way, you will be that much better equipped to fully enjoy your daily activities and feel the energetic benefits of living life with passion. For the love of yourself and your life, Lighten up!

Make an official decision

No ifs, ands or buts, you are going to do it! This is the exact kind of mental attitude a passionate person has about their decisions in life. Procrastination kills the energy in just about any good intention, and what's more, indecision literally puts a halt to all good things. Decide now, once and for all, that you will live passionately and on purpose. All great action, all great experience, came from a great decision. Decide, and don't look back!

Like everything in life, the more you give of yourself in a focused and intentional fashion, the more you get out of that which you are giving to. I invite you to give yourself wholly to the process you are about to embark on - Living a passionate life!

4 Common Traps to Avoid

S o! You want to find your passion? Well done! This is an exciting journey, but beware! There are many dangerous traps along the way to your goal! Or maybe you have just found your passion - congratulations. You are one step closer to living your dream! But before you go rushing off to enjoy your new found exciting love, or before you charge off on your journey of self discovery, you will need to consider a few things carefully to avoid dire ruin.

While you are on this journey, you will want this guide of potential traps so you know what to watch out for and avoid those pitfalls. Here's Part 1 of what you'll need to think about: the first four pitfalls when you actively try to find your passion.

The D.E.A.R trap

The first dangerous trap you can fall into! Sounds like a literal trap doesn't it? But DEAR Trap actually stands for Dropping Everything And Running TowaRds A Passion!

Does this warning sound backwards to you? Once you find your passion, you should put aside your fears and immediately run at it full steam, right?

Wrong. First, you need to think.

Maybe your new passion is a business. Great. But do you need to quit your job immediately? Do your research - maybe you need to wait 6 months to get all the licences you need - maybe renovating that new shop space for your dream store is going to take a few months or a year! Will you be able to cope without income for that long? How will your mortgage go during that time? Your kids?

The D.E.A.R. trap reminds us that even when we are passionate, we need to keep our eyes open, consider our situation, and move carefully, so we don't find our life trapped by what we hold dear.

The Passion Pit

What is The Passion Pit? Does it describe your current job perhaps? A dark hole where passion is sent to die?

I honestly pray this is not the case for anyone reading this. But if it is, I can understand why you might be trying to find your passion!

Trap 2, the Passion Pit, comes about when we assume that our passion is a viable business, when it really doesn't need to be. Your passion could be a completely fulfilling hobby!

To illustrate the danger of assuming Passion = Profit, allow me to use a local example. Maybe you really love belly dancing, as a local business owner in my area does. But does that mean you should spend $3,000 a week in shop-front rent to open a belly dancing supply store? If you live in a small town/suburb, where belly dancers are few (or none at all!)? the answer is no. The business I referred to went broke in 4 months. Not only are there few dancers in this area, but from my limited understanding of belly dancers, they don't need a lot of gear either!

Now, there may be a market for belly dancing gear if this person had built their business online, but there isn't a market here in my local area. So, do what this person should have done first: think about whether your passion is genuinely profitable, and if so, consider if your initial expression of that business idea is also profitable.

Seek advice from experts, not just supportive friends/family. Don't allow your passion to become a money pit of a business if it isn't meant to be a business at all. Because that money pit has every chance of sucking your passion in with it.

Rotten Fruit

Ok. So you've found your passion, and now you want to do it all the time - because that will make you happy, right? Well, sometimes the answer is no. The third trap to beware of is Rotten Fruit.

Not all passions are good for you. What is the fruit of your passion? Maybe your passion is fine whiskey. What would be the fruit of trying to drink fine whiskey all day? Poverty? Almost certainly alcoholism - perhaps even liver failure or death.

A healthy passion does not necessarily produce healthy fruit if you try to do it all day. Be wary of any passion that threatens your health or liberty - especially if you decide your passion is something that is also illegal. Sometimes, depending on the passion, you may be happier in a life that doesn't include a huge amount of your passion. When considering a passion, consider the healthiest expression of that passion. Perhaps with fine whiskey, it is publishing a book or blog on the topic?

The Passion Dash

The fourth trap to avoid falling into is rushing to the conclusion that you only have one passion.

Maybe you have read the first few traps through, and realised that not all passions are profitable, or healthy. Well, if yours is one of these, it is not hopeless.

You may have several passions! Am I wrong? You tell me! Do you have one friend, or do you have more than one? Do you only love one of your children?

Love doesn't run out when we use it, and we can love more than one thing. To illustrate, consider the movie Chariots of Fire, based on the lives of Harold Abrahams and Eric Liddell at the 1924 Paris Olympics. Both men had a passion for running, but for Abrahams, that run was "10 seconds to justify my whole existence." Heavy. Whereas for Liddell, his passions in life were

1. Being a Missionary in China, and also

2. Running.

Two strong passions. Did having two passions make Liddell weaker than Abrahams? On the contrary. Both men were passionate runners, and both men won their Olympic events. But one gold medallist (according to the movie) spent only 10 seconds justifying his existence, and the other, spent a lifetime in China justifying his, working on his other passion. So remember Eric Liddell's Passion Dash. Don't live for 10 seconds only. Look for ALL your passions.

Putting it Into Practice

There comes a time in everyone's life when passion screams to be released, demonstrated, or put to active use.

There's a sense of "Something's missing" and it must be discovered. Becoming cognizant of your passion may require inquisitive actions, but will prove to be well worth the quest. Once unleashed, passion can bring the most fulfillment in life.

So what is passion? Passion is what brings you the most satisfaction. Passion is your zeal personified. Passion denotes a great fondness or intense interest. Passion is what makes you shine and stand out like the brightest crayon in the box. Paycheck or no paycheck, passion is what you are willing to do with a smile on your face in the absence of being paid to do it. Passion is directly linked to your purpose and success in life. It helps to completes you; however, it is not to be confused with a person's gifts, talents, skills, or abilities.

Think back to your earliest memories as a child growing up. What thoughts immediately come to mind? Were you the adventuresome kind that one day wanted to become a firefighter or a policeman? Ladies, did you line your dolls up and teach them Math or English? What was your earliest desire to become in life? What could you be found doing on rainy or snowy days? These questions may provide clues to tapping into your passion.

Day in and day out, countless numbers of women and men go to work faithfully to support themselves and their families. Their gifts, talents, skills, and abilities are used in support of companies' visions. Passion, for many, is "on hold" as the primary focus becomes "working for a living." While working to meet fundamental needs are honorable, and keeps food on the table and a roof overhead, what about your passion?

Is it possible to ignore your passion, as if it does not exist? In answer to this question, your passion has bounce back, resilience ability. No matter how hard you or others may try to snuff your passion out, it always resurfaces anew! Why, because it defines you. Your passion is directly connected to your purpose in life. It cannot be ignored forever. Left unaddressed, there will be times when the flames of passion will be fanned, renewing the zeal within. It may lie dormant for a season, but it does not disappear.

There are those who have already identified their passions. They can be found operating in one aspect or another of their fondest interests. For others, passion has to be discovered and identified. Unveiling passion is a process which requires reflection, acknowledgement, and execution.

Reflection: While it may not be the easiest thing to do, seek quiet times and places to spend quality time thinking and reflecting on personal interests. Revisit those childhood dreams. This is a good time to do some journaling, affording you the opportunity to capture your thoughts on paper. List things you enjoy doing - things that bring a smile to your face, as well as a sense of pleasure and satisfaction.

Ask yourself the question, "If money was not an issue, what would I like to be found doing?" Soliciting the help of family, friends, and co-workers may be beneficial in composing your list. Once your list is complete, narrow your list by drawing a line through items of less significance until you are able to determine with confidence, what your passion is.

Acknowledge: Once identified, acknowledge and research your passion. Keep up the journal entries as you continue this process of self-discovery. Brainstorm ways of implementing your passion into your life. Draw mindmaps, pouring all your ideas around your newfound passion onto paper. How have others successfully accomplished this? Share your newly discovered passion with others who can appreciate your excitement. This could lead to more insight and ideas.

Execute. By now you have discovered and acknowledged your passion. Great job! So, what's next? Execution, follow through is your next step. Set a course of action in place to make room for your passion. Spend time in prayer and meditation for your next steps. Set goals with a series of actions steps in place. You didn't stop journaling, right? Capture your goals and success plan on paper.

You may want to also consider partnering with a life coach or mentor. The role of the life coach will provide the support, encouragement, and accountability you may need in successfully implementing your passion. A good life coach will help develop the leader within you. The role of a mentor will provide someone with the experience within your field of interest. A good mentor will impart wisdom and direction.

FIND YOUR PASSION

We're all wired with passion. Identifying that passion and flowing in it leads to a sense of completeness and satisfaction. Unveil your passion through the process of reflection, acknowledgement, and execution. Be ready to shine as the brightest crayon in the box.

THE 3 KEYS TO A FULFILLING LIFE

Life without passion is like college without the diploma. Passion is the driving force of life, thrusting us along in rolling waves. We have all ridden the waves of passion. More than that, we have all wished to be them.

You have seen them, have you not? In politics, during church, on the stage – those people who do not ride the waves of passion. They make them. Have we not wished to be them? Or to hold that passion within us?

It would be abnormal if we did not long to be consumed with a passion-filled life. That is because we were made for a passion-filled life. Sometimes it comes to us – through a sunset, a first kiss, a sermon. And at those times, how can we not help but desire to hold this passion with us forever?

The 3 keys to a passion-filled life are available to everyone because everyone is made to create waves of overwhelming inspiration out of life. The keys are easy. More importantly, the keys are natural to us. Performing them is like receiving that college diploma after four years of grueling work.

Those who can make waves out of life understand the basic principle of a passion-filled life

Our passion can only consume us if it comes from something greater than who we are.

How do we find this? How do we learn a passion that is greater than who we are?

Worship.

Worship is the act of fervently saying thank you. Every human has the desire, the impulse, to worship. Whenever we do enter into the act of worship, we become a part of, and build a connection to, who we worship.

To be entirely consumed is to find something beyond ourselves. If we want to find the highest degree of a passion-filled life, then our worship must be of a highest degree. This requires asking what is the highest degree.

Well, put simply, God is the highest. So in order to become a part of the highest degree, we must connect with Him. And in order to be filled with the highest passion, worship to God must take place.

When we do worship God in acts of fervent praise, we connect with Him. This connection allows Him to fill us with passion. Without that worship, the connection, and thus the passion, would never become a part of us.

One of my dear friends once told me, "Passion is impossible without compassion."

I believe this to be true with every part of my being. In order to live a passion-filled life, we must develop:

A compassion.

Why? Because passion takes heart. It takes a love so strung that hundreds of carving knives can never cut the strings of our passion. That is what a passion-filled life takes. If we do not hold onto keeping the fires of compassion burning bright, then our passion may never grow to its fullest potential.

People can be passionate about many things. All of us hold a passion for at least one thing. Though when the end comes, they seem to just come up short.

Sunset turns to night. Our first kiss turns to a second. Sermons are left in the wake for next service. The passion is cut short. How, then, do we keep our passion from fraying and find a compassion that will last?

There are two things on this Earth that will not turn to dust:

• God

• People

God will last forever, and though people's bodies turn to dust, their spirits will live on for eternity.

Life is about more than coming up short. If we want this passion-filled existence, then it is time to develop a heart for God and His people. That compassion is the only compassion that will not drown in the waves. That compassion will fill us so deep, we will overrun with it, until finally, it begins to touch others.

That, is how waves are made.

3. Even if we do achieve a consuming passion, what is the point if we do nothing with it?

Plan.

The final key to a passion-filled life is to plan to touch the lives of people. The greatest plan is one that extends out beyond ourselves. Plan to work outside the spheres you have always known because that is all you can ever do. We limit ourselves to what surrounds us until we put ourselves in a place where we may expand.

There is an entire world who longs to touch the waves of passion your life can produce, and as you reach out to them, you expand your own heart, your own self, and your own passion. Then, you have become greater than yourself because you have made waves that are not the product of your compassion, but of God's unlimited passion-filled sea.

Passion Management – A New way Of Getting Things done

P assion Management acknowledges that we do, indeed, have multiple passions. I, for one, always refer to myself as a multi-passionate entrepreneur and person. Also, Passion Management is a much more positive way of describing our dilemma of what to do with all of these great ideas. Time management and project management are terms that are not only overused, but unfortunately, can be a negative reminders of our lack of time, as opposed to a motivating factor that leads to productivity.

Passion Management is the ability to manage all of the passions you want to tackle in business and life. Here are some tips to help guide your Passion Management.

Pick a Passion

Most multi-passionate people are swimming in a sea of great ideas, and often have the drive to make them happen. The conundrum is which passion to pursue. My advice – pick a passion and go for it! Author and life coach Cheryl Richardson talked about this when I heard her speak in NYC years ago. She said that so many of her clients get stuck because they have so many great ideas and passions, but don't know which to pursue. So they wind up pursuing... yup, you guessed it – nothing.

Don't fall victim to passion confusion! It is better to pick a passion and allow it to blossom and flourish than to be trapped under a mountain of too many great ideas. If you pick a passion and it does not go well or does not take off the way you wanted it to, that's okay. Regroup, learn from your passion exercise, and pick a new one.

Tap Into Your Passion

One of the best ways to determine what you should (and want to) focus on is to tap into your passion. Sometimes we lose focus with our business or personal projects and we need to take the time to remind ourselves what we value and why we are staying the course. It is all too easy to get bogged down in details and tasks. Try to ask yourself, "Why am I really doing this project?" and see if there is a reason that relates back to one of your passions, whether personal or professional.

For example, maybe you are feeling the crunch of trying to blog several times a week. Ask yourself why you set this schedule and whether it taps into one of your passions. If your passion is to write, then write! Do you need to stay on a particular schedule? Will anyone but you notice if you only write when your passion strikes? Sometimes we set ourselves up for failure, or more likely, undue stress, when we remain too regimented.

Yes, I am a professional organizer and see the value in systems, processes, and timelines, trust me. But it is vital to check in and ask yourself: "Is this tapping into my passion?" If so, it will help propel you forward and remind you why you are doing this particular task or project. If you realize this task or project does not tap into any of your passions, you may decide to abandon the project, delegate the task, or reevaluate whether you want and need to continue it.

Ignore the Naysayers

Often, you are making actual progress towards achieving your passions, but someone tries to sabotage you. Try not to let this derail your efforts! You need to stay the course, despite what they say. If you are truly passionate about the project, you will be able to withstand attacks. The famous life coach Martha Beck talks about surrounding yourself with people who can be your "believing eyes."

I love this idea! Adopt it and use it as your own. Stay away from the Negative Nellies, and surround yourself with people who believe in your passionate goals and will help you achieve them. Passion is contagious and can not only serve as strong motivation for you, but as inspiration for others. People notice passion. In fact, in my opinion, people often notice passion more than they notice productivity!

Celebrate Your Passion Successes

When we take on a project or task and successfully complete it, we often reward ourselves at the completion. But when we pursue a passion, we may not have any reward system built-in. In some situations, it is hard to determine when we have "completed" a passion. Passions are often ongoing. They can be a particular way of approaching a topic, or a passion can be a mindset or belief.

But it is important to come up with some way of rewarding your successes and milestones when pursuing your passions. Figure out ways to evaluate whether you have achieved a certain level of success for a particular passion. The more successful you feel at each step, the more apt you are to keep moving on the path towards achieving your passion goals. And most passionate people just want to keep the passion going!

Get down everything you've been thinking about lately that you want to learn or work on. Note: This is not a commitment to do all or even one of those things. It's just a way to let yourself see it. That's all. Once you see it, you might have something that's just begging to be done or tried. Just listen to it, OK? Promise?

Make it easy. A lot of my clients mention that, once they put hours into commuting, working at a soul-sucking job, & making & eating dinner, they can barely do anything but sit on the couch & watch Judge Judy reruns (not that there is anything remotely wrong with that – it's how I start each weekday!). How can you get your pep back? Make it easy.

For example, if you already know you want to paint but are having trouble getting motivated to go into your studio, how can you make it as easy as possible to start? Maybe, before you leave for work that morning, you setup your paints & take out the photo that serves as your inspiration so all you need to do is open the door & you'll be ready to go.

Is there a weekly or monthly commitment you feel you "have" to go to? Then say "no" or delegate it to someone else, & claim your time for yourself. Know that post-work time is a lost cause? Set your alarm 30 minutes early & use that time to do what you want to do (I won't dare say "for your passion!"). It's all about finding the right structure & shortcuts for you, so experiment!

Don't think beyond right now. Once you start thinking about picking the "passion" that you'll be bound to (gulp) forever, the Vampires are gonna come creeping in. Listen, nobody has a crystal ball, so who the heck knows where you'll be or what you'll want to be doing in another year, let alone another 50? So let's take those questions above and add "right now" to the end (i.e. "What do I do for fun right now?" or "What gives me energy right now?" or "What do I like learning about right now?"). The one exception is that you can think of things in the past that you enjoyed / gave you energy / liked learning about, so feel free to replace the "do" with "did."

The Fuel Human Beings Use

C hildren focus fiercely on everything they do while doing it. Nothing else exists. The world is just them and whatever it is they are doing at that moment: the game they are playing, the movie they are watching, the toy they are holding... And with that focus comes passion, their inexhaustible source of energy. But then we grow...

As we grow, our attention is divided into a million needs and tasks. We rarely just do one single thing at a time and most of what we do doesn't even require our full attention. We learn to shift our focus from one problem to the next, from one action to the next or back to the previous one. We forget the art of just being totally immersed in only one task, in flow with it, unaware and uncaring about anything else. And as we do, our energy spreads to feed and fuel that myriad of smaller actions we undertake. No wonder why we never feel energetic enough anymore!

Passion is the fuel for human energy. We see it in children, but also in those few adults who still maintain their passion for what they do. Have you ever met anybody truly passionate about something who complains of a lack of energy? Just the opposite, right? Those you meet who seem to never tire are profoundly passionate about what they do. Without passion, energy dwindles and it does so because passion requires focus so the three go together and feed one another: passion, focus, energy.

Many people come to me because they feel exhausted and without energy or because they can't perform at the level they see me or others performing. 'What's your secret?' they ask me. 'How can you have so much energy?' The answer is my passion. I passionately love what I do: I passionately love writing and speaking, interacting with other human beings, getting to know them... I passionately love being alive. When those people come to me, they never have a passion of their own and without it, there is no focus.

Think about it for a moment. Look back onto your childhood or just observe children at play. When playing, nothing else exists; just the game. Do you remember that feeling of utter concentration and devotion? That is what you're missing. You go to work but are you fully there? I bet you aren't. Or you only are for short bouts of time. That's why those who professionally devote themselves to their passion never look tired. Unfortunately, most human beings just have a job, not a passion.

Most people just do their jobs or pursue their career not because it's a passion for them, but for many other reasons. They might choose certain studies based on the greater probabilities to find a job later on, or the amount of money they will bring them, or who knows what. And that is OK, as long as they also realize that days will feel long and boring and will always be accompanied by that perennial feeling of exhaustion.

I feel like this is a rule of life: passion transforms into energy; a lack of passion results in a lack of energy. As simple as that. If you want to feel more energetic in life, you're going to have to change the way you live to find more passion or to create more opportunities to feel passionate about something.

Let me offer you some tips on how to turn a job into something you might feel passionate for. (You can also quit your current job and follow your passion, if you have one, of course, but this next section is for those who already have a job, no specific passion and can't just shift careers at present.) So, if you are a manager in a company, for example, and feel like working days completely drain you of your energy, ask yourself what in your job sparks your passion... Nothing? Very little? Why doesn't it surprise me? Let's try and create or ignite some passion in you, then.

Go over the list of tasks you perform on a regular week and try and find something in them that you could eventually feel passionate about; human interaction, reaching excellence, being the best at one aspect of your work, creativity, productivity... or maybe even reaching the next wrung in the ladder... whatever.

Once you find it, start devoting your full attention to that goal on incremental steps: first 10 minutes a day, then 15, then 20, and so on. Those minutes need to be like children at play, absolutely focused and devoted. If distracted, go back to the task and focus on the positives it brings you. Think about what it is you enjoy about them, how they make you feel, what is that interests you when performing them. Focus on them at the moment, not on what they might bring in the future.

While performing other tasks that are not the ones you identified as possible sources of passion, try to focus your full attention on each of them while carrying them out; a bit like mindful working. When changing tasks, shift your full attention to the new task at hand.

If you can't seem to be able to fully focus on something, ask yourself what part of that specific task is distracting you, or which other task is so important that it keeps calling your attention onto it. Focus on that one aspect or task, get it out of the way, so to speak, and go back to focusing on one task at a time.

Once you feel a spark of passion for any of the tasks you perform, no matter how big or small, look for similar tasks in your job or possible new developments related to that one task that could open new avenues or result in more opportunities to do what you just discovered you love doing. If necessary, talk to your superiors and let them know about your passion. Managers know passionate employees always yield better results, so chances are they might give you a few more shots at advancing along those lines.

If nothing you do at work sparks your passion at all, apply all 5 points above to your personal life... what do you do outside of work that sparks your passion? And focus on those instead, to build a life of meaning and energy for yourself.

So, do you have any passions in your life? What gets you excited or moving? Use that! Because a life without passion is like a movie in slow motion; nice and fun to watch for a short while, but quite boring after a long while.

Unlocking the Passion Paradox

I n my opinion, passion is one of the most attractive qualities a person can possess. When you are passionate about something, others are drawn to you; you are able to influence more effectively and lead more successfully. Beyond these interpersonal facts, there are valuable personal benefits for possessing passion in your life.

When we are passionate we are more productive, happier, healthier, have more energy, less stress, higher work/life satisfaction and typically a better attitude about everything in our lives. Which highlights what I call The Passion Paradox – passion is great, but what do you do when you just aren't feeling passionate about much of anything?

It is a common challenge, and why I call it a paradox. Passion is something we want, but we don't always know how or where to find it. Actually, part of the answer comes in that last sentence. Here's that part again: "... we don't know how or where to find it." Most people are waiting for passion to find them, or on a situation, job or relationship to bring them passion.

When the benefits are so great – why should you wait? You'll begin to unlock the passion paradox when you go looking for the passion(s) in your life – being proactive – rather than waiting for them to find us. So if you find yourself feeling frustrated, despondent or generally not feeling very inspired or passionate about things, go on a "passion hunt" with one or more of the following ideas:

Look for good

Things in your life or in your job might not be great right now; passion low or nonexistent. The outlook might seem a little bleak, or the job doesn't "do anything" for you, but part of that is up to you. What are you looking for? Are you becoming cynical or focusing on the things you don't like? Start looking for the good in your situation – even super, small good things. Once you get your mind looking for the good, you will begin to find it. Overtime, this habit will help you find wonderful things – if you continually look for the good.

Look to serve

When you are serving, helping or encouraging others, passion will often arrive. Find service opportunities in your current situations or find ways to volunteer your time and talents. You might be surprised how fast passion arrives when you look to serve.

Look at the big picture

You'll be able to put your problems and challenges in context when you take a minute to consider the big picture. Hopefully taking a longer view will help put things in a more proper perspective and show that the current challenges and frustrations that seem to be sapping your passion are temporary. You will often find your passion when you look at the big picture.

Look at your attitude

When your attitude is more positive it is easier to feel passionate, find passion and attract passion. The opposite is also true. Your attitude is your choice. Are you choosing the attitude that is conducive to finding your passion? If you want more passion in your life, look at your attitude.

Look in other parts of your life

Maybe passion is lacking in one part of your life. If so, look elsewhere. Remind yourself of and immerse yourself in a hobby. Find the passion in other areas of your life (other than work, as an example). You may not, in every minute of your life, have passion in all of your life, so look to other areas to find and feed your passions.

Look at your choices. Bottom line?

We all have choices to make that will impact the amount of passion in our lives. Each of the other suggestions above have an element of choice in them. If you want more passion in your life, take responsibility for the choices you make. If you want to find passion, look at your choices.

Will these things guarantee passion in your life tomorrow? No. (But you might be surprised how quickly things will change for you when you start looking.) That however is not the most useful question to be asking right now. The more productive question is: What am I willing to do to put more passion into my life? Opening your eyes and beginning to look in the ways I've suggested are all proactive ways to begin rekindling or evening finding your passion. As with most things, when you actually look, you'll have a much great chance of finding. Happy hunting!

The 75/25 Rule

H ave you ever heard of the 75/25 rule? If not, it's not surprising – a lot of people haven't. But, it's really one of the basic tenements on the road to learning how to find your passion.

Finding Your Passion: The 75/25 Rule Explained

The rule itself is quite simple. It's this – spend three-quarters of your time on your strengths, and only a quarter on your weaknesses. The reason this is so powerful is that it allows you to focus the majority of your efforts on things you're not only good at, but happy doing.

Why What Some Consider Your Strengths Can Really Be a Weakness

You see, you can be good at something, but it can still be a weakness. Why? Because if you're good at something, but don't enjoy it, how effective are you likely to be at it day in and day out?

Where Many of Us Go Wrong When We're Trying to Find Our Passion

The number one mistake I see in my success coaching business that prevents many from finding their passion is that they spend their energies on the wrong things. Usually, it's because of a couple of reasons.

They think it's because they think it's what they should be doing: Most of us never stop to question the status quo. So if you own an online PR business, for example, and everyone says you have to be active on social media, but you hate social media, how happy do you think you're going to be engaging in it?

Not only will you be unhappy, the return on your efforts won't be nearly what they would be if you enjoyed this activity. So, does this mean you should give up on social media? No – and that's the point of using the 75/25 rule.

You figure out what your strengths are so you can focus on them – and find other ways to get done what you're not good at and/or don't enjoy doing.

For example, in this case you might outsource your social media marketing to a freelancer. It keeps your business front and center, and leaves you to focus on what you enjoy most – interacting with your PR clients and finding different stories to pitch to the media to get them that all-important coverage.

Fear – this is perhaps the main reason many waste their energies on their weaknesses.

Many of my clients initially come to me desperately unhappy. They may have the trappings of success – e.g., a good job, making great money, on a high-flying success track – but inside, they're miserable.

And it's because they're afraid of making a change. Fear keeps many locked into utilizing 75 percent of their energy on their weaknesses – instead of their strengths – because they're afraid to make a change.

This is totally understandable because there can be a lot to lose. However, once I explain to them how to find their passion by tapping into their strengths, it's like their fear just melts away.

Finding Your Passion: Getting on the Road to Success Begins with Knowing

Let me draw a line for you – when you know what you're put here to do (what your purpose in life is), bad habits like procrastination disappear. This is because you're in love; you're passionate about what you're doing. Then, you're more successful because it's not a chore; you pour in the hours.

Your success gives you more confidence, which leads to more opportunities and more success because you operate from a place of "I can," instead of "I can't," or "What if," or "Maybe I shouldn't."

And this is what tapping into your strengths – and spending the majority of your time working in this zone – can do for you.

I've seen it time and time and time again in my success coaching business. Once I show my clients how to how to tap into their strengths, it's like a whole new world opens up. This is the power – and reward – of tapping into your strengths to find your passion.

7 Secrets to Discover Your Purpose

D o you ever wonder, "What on Earth am I here for?" Maybe you've tried your hand at various things, and each time you've felt engaged for a while, but eventually you lose interest and boredom sets in.

That's exactly what one of my clients was going through. He attempted to go back to college on several occasions, but never completed more than a semester or two. He wanted to go back to college and complete a major once and for all, but he couldn't figure out what his passion was.

Are you going through a similar situation? If you've tried many things to no great success, then here's what you need to know.

First of all, I believe you already have part of your answer. You know what you are inclined towards, and I'm sure you've got a pretty good idea as to what you aren't passionate about as well, which would be the majors that you've tried but didn't like in the past.

I strongly recommend finding your passion first, and then choosing the best outlet for your passion. The best way I've found to discover your passion is a combination of getting to know yourself and exposing yourself to new situations.

Passion is all about who you are and what you're wired to do. If you don't know your passion then it's wise to ask yourself some specific questions to gather some clues.

Ask yourself, what is it that you really enjoy about the activities you love and the topics you're interested in? What is it about them that really engages you? Is there anything else that takes up the bulk of your time and interest that you've missed? What is it about those things you enjoy? What is it you don't enjoy about what you are doing right now? And what is it you enjoy, and didn't enjoy about the majors you've taken in the past?

Gather all these answers together and come up with a list of things you haven't tried yet based on them. Then devote a good part of your time to read up, experiment and experience these activities. Each time you try a new activity, use the questions I shared to analyze your experiences and come up with new ideas and activities to try.

As you go through this process, you will be able to find your passion, and more importantly you'll truly know yourself and broaden your horizons in the process. And then I believe you'll have a clear idea of what to do with your life.

Are you living your purpose and sharing your passion while being handsomely rewarded for doing it? I am. You? This week's topic is all about discovering your purpose and getting paid for your passion. Today, I'm so excited to share with you my seven simple secrets to discover your purpose and get paid for your passion.

Now, you may have heard the term. "Do your life's work, and the money will come." Or "Do what makes you happy" You've probably heard this before, but you're also probably not sure exactly how living your purpose fits in to your business, let alone how to get paid for your passion.

Allow me to share my insights on 'WHAT' you must know to discover your purpose and get paid for your passion. 'WHY' you must get paid for living the life you were meant to live, and the number one thing that's holding you back. If you ever wondered why you're not making more in your business and have had the suspicion you're currently not doing the work you're here to do, you are in for a REAL treat. I promise!

I truly believe getting crystal clear on your purpose and passion can change everything about your business and life. Everyone has something special and that makes you stand out from others. So "Do what makes you happy."

Let's paint the big picture together for a moment. Imagine a mountain – let's call it a Magic Mountain, with a CASTLE at the top. And you are in your "soul searching" journey. There are different learning experiences, life lessons. You are at the bottom, in your comfort zone. The next level up is the "confusion" zone and then the next level up comes the "clarity." The key point is that you can't live your purpose if you don't learn your life's lesson.

Now your business is an expression of your purpose. So to get paid for your passion, you absolutely must have a business that expresses your purpose, and it really is that specific.

Remember it's the inner work that creates the outer experience, not the other way around. If there is a struggle on the outside, there is a struggle on the inside. And we are either moving up or moving down. It's very important for you to step back from your life and go, "Why am I doing these things? What am I hoping to gain? How do I bring a spiritual piece, meaning the mind-set, heart-set, soul-set and Universal principles, into my own business?" So, let's dig a little bit deeper.

7 Simple Secrets to Discover Your Purpose and Get Paid For Your Passion
Decide what you don't want

You must have 'Clarity of Intention' because when you do, the Universe conspires with you to make it happen. And the best way to figure out what you want is to figure out what you DON'T want first. The biggest challenge is that most people don't: #1. Dream BIG enough, #2. Know what they want, and #3. Most people are not clear enough in ASKING. So decide what you don't want today.

What do you TRULY want?

Take into account some practical considerations. Get clear on "Where do you live? How much do you make? What do you do?" And the meaningful considerations: "What difference do you make? What is your legacy? What are you remembered for?"

To help you go deeper here, let's play the 'Billionaire Game.' Imagine your IDEAL Life 3 years from now. In all areas: financial, professional, personal, physical, social, emotional, spiritual, relationships, family, contribution, and so forth. You get the picture. Make a list of all the things you DO want. For example, what you like/love to do now (that you are a billionaire).

What activity makes you the happiest? If time and money were not factors, what would you most like to study and/or learn how to do? What is your dream? What is your big goal? What is it you really want in life? What is the most important to you? What's your highest value? Get clear on all these things. Clarity is really important. In business, Clarity = Clients! The critical key here is to align with your passion and purpose.

What's your BIG why behind it all?

Know WHY you want this. "Until thought is linked with purpose there is no intelligent accomplishment." – James Allen, As A Man Thinketh

WARNING: Be careful about the big WHY behind it all wanting money for money's sake is not the same as saying, "Universe, I know I am here for a HIGHER purpose and I am overjoyed to accomplish this task, but I need lots of help to make manifest this vision."

Here's a hint to help you. Pay close attention to what section of the bookstore you gravitate to and what books are on your bookshelf. Go even deeper, ask yourself and be totally honest: "What stirs your soul? What makes your heart beat faster and stronger? What inspires you? What really makes you get out of the bed in the morning? What are you most proud of having accomplished at this point in your life?" And above all, define success. What does success mean to you? It's all part of the process. Listen to the answers you're getting and trust the process. Let your passion and purpose unfold!

What are YOU passionate about? What are your true passions?

What challenges might your passion help you to overcome? How will your passion contribute to the desires and needs of others? Will this passion move you toward your purpose in life? If so how?

What would you do for Free, all day long, and still feel passionate about?

Here's a clue: What gives you untold energy when you do it? You'll want to describe your "Perfect Day" – If you had all the money you needed, where and how would you live? If your answer is: "I don't know." Take a moment to get some momentum and some inspiring ideas. Find out: Who inspires you and why? Who is your Role Model and Why? Who in history do you admire most, and Why? How can you become more like this person?

What do you want to leave for others after you are gone? Be specific.

In other words, what do you want for yourself, for others, for life personally? What is truly most important to you? What do you want, professionally, for your clients, community and the world? Why do you do what you do? What do you offer that is unique and/or excites you? At the end of your life, what do you think you would most regret not having done for yourself?

What is a dream or goal you've given up on?

Look back in time and be aware of what goal or part of your life you've put on the back burner because the 'time isn't right,' and what part of you is just waiting for the right person and/or the right opportunity to catalyze it.

Make a decision and declare it. Believe it's on its way. Let go of obstacles to your believing. Just believe. Watch for signs and happy coincidences. Take action on signs and opportunities. *"Whatever you can do or dream you can, begin it! Boldness has genius, power, and magic in it."* – Goethe

When you discover your purpose and you express that through your business, you start getting paid for your passion. It helps you to keep focused on what you really want. You become who you dream of being – the best version of your authentic you – avoiding all that self-doubt and negativity.

Once we get to the Clarity, it's fabulous. Our purpose is what comes most easily to us. Each of us is unique and different, and for myself, when I recognized this, I literally designed my yearly authentic business success road map aligned with my passion and purpose. It makes all the difference in the world. Now I'm really focused and I truly don't invest my time, energy and money in things that don't have some specific link to living my purpose and sharing what I'm passionate about.

Authentic Business Success In Action

Get crystal clear and focus on what you truly want. "Where attention goes, energy flows." In growing your authentic business success as an enlightened entrepreneur to the next level, like I am doing now, you get that you will have resistance if you keep doing it the way you have been doing it. You need to walk more towards your passion and purpose, and when you do, things unfold so quickly and so beautifully that it's shocking sometimes how fast things happen.

Say 'YES' to living your purpose and get paid for your passion. Get focused and start designing your own authentic business success road map that you can follow right away. But don't take my word for it. The only way you are going to find out is to experience it. That's the ONLY way. Experience it. What that feels like.

A final word of wisdom: "Creation works with joy, not negativity." If your inner voice is negative, you instantly know it's NOT truth. This is a mindset issue. And this mindset challenge is what separates fulfilled and successful entrepreneurs from unfulfilled and unsuccessful entrepreneurs, because those who are fulfilled and successful are willing to do 'the work' while the unfulfilled and unsuccessful ones are not. And this is where mindset comes in. As they say, "When you are interested, you do what's convenient, but when you're committed, you do whatever it takes."

When you are committed to living your purpose through your business, and when you do so, you immediately step into the bigger version of yourself, which means you serve so many more people on Earth, and therefore you are handsomely rewarded for it. When you do that you are fulfilling your purpose, sharing your passion, achieving your dreams and you are saying 'YES' to the opportunity – all while getting paid for it. And that's when MAGIC happens. Magic happens when you are building a thriving, profitable, successful business while being authentic and aligned with your passion and purpose.

However, there is one thing that could be holding you back. And that is the number one obstacle entrepreneurs face: that's F.E.A.R. (False Evidence Appearing Real). Fear of Success or Fear of Failure, Fear of doing the wrong thing right now. The best news is you can never be doing the wrong thing. It's always an alignment. Everything is leading you to your purpose.

So discover your unique purpose and get paid for your passion because once you know it you can't not know it. And you start being in alignment with everything you do both professionally and personally. And this is what I call Authentic Business Success as an Enlightened Entrepreneur. And this is why I created the seven simple secrets I've been revealing to you so you too can discover your purpose and get paid for your passion.

"God's gift to you is more talent and ability than you could possibly use in your lifetime. Your gift to God is to develop as much of that talent and ability as you can in this lifetime." – Steve Bow

"What your mind can dream up can absolutely become a reality."

Just one more thing. And it's about the 'HOW' because we've talked about the 'WHAT' and 'WHY.' You don't need to worry about the 'HOW.' Most people don't make a decision until they see the 'how.' But the 'how' doesn't show up until you make that decision.

"Do not worry about how. It is all taken care of for you as long as you do your part of thinking, acting, speaking and being in accordance with that dream. Just dream, visualize, and then start doing something. Do the next thing that you feel you should do in accordance with that dream, and keep moving. The little that you do triggers something else you had not foreseen and on and on this goes until it completes." – David Cameron Gikandi

Ways to Discover More Passion In Your Life

Create a Board

Creating a passion board, also known as a vision board, can be very powerful. This is especially effective if you are a highly-visual person. Creating a passion board is easy. Find and clip out images, symbols and words that represent the essence of each of your passions. Make a collage and only add an item to it if it absolutely evokes a strong and powerful emotion within. Keep this in a place where you and only you will see it. Locations you frequent often such as your closet or personal bathroom are ideal locations for most people.

Create a Statement

A passion statement is not an absolute defining rule for you or anybody else to live by. In fact it is unnecessary to create rules in your life or the life of others... unless, of course, this is your rule. Passion is something that doesn't need to be ruled into existence, it needs to be discovered.

Where do you adventure with yourself today? On a 3'x5' index card begin to craft your passion statement. It could be whatever you feel at this point in your life gives you meaning, how you make sense of the world, an aim to focus, or an ideal to pursue. For best results you should revise at will and revisit this often, even daily if possible.

Reflect on Your Passions

Try writing your personal affirmations and/or most passion words on your personal bathroom mirror with the same pens they use for white boards. These 'dry-erase' markers make for easy cleaning when your ready to change or tweak your words. A good thing to use if you cannot find words to write is your passion statement. Read your power phrases daily as you brush your teeth and get ready for the day in the morning. Read the mirror again as you wash up and get ready for bed. Experiment with different colors combinations until your passion appears both appealing and attractive.

Practice Gratitude Passionately

Passion comes alive where gratitude thrives. If you appreciate the ability or opportunity to do something you automatically do it with more love and attention. Write out your top 5 passions on 3'x5' index cards. Start with the words "I am so happy and grateful to be now..." or "I am so grateful now that..." then list 5 of your life's passion. Don't list them unless they make you feel incredible just thinking about them. Practice the feeling of having them. Underneath write "This or something greater now manifests for the good of all concerned." Place them strategically in your home, car, or carry them with you. Practice pulling them out often, especially whenever you feel ungrateful or down in the dumps.

Make Passionate Sleep

Your sleep is most likely the most important part of your passion equation. Passion brings out the best in you but if you have absolutely no energy then it is impossible to function at your best. To be your best you need proper rest. Be passionate about solving your sleep puzzle.

What will it take for you to get an incredible night's sleep every night. Start experimenting with different things that might work. What might a sleep mask, music, ear plugs, hot tea, or warm bath do for you? Begin making small modifications at a time. Small changes can make a big impact on your overall sleep.

Build a Passion Support Team

The people you surround yourself has a bigger part to play in discovering and living your passions then you might think. A big mistake that people make is trying to discover their passions all alone. Passion is something that is meant to be shared and discovered with others. Find and surround yourself with people of vision and like-mind. Be sure to befriend people who have already pursued their passions with success. Check out groups and associations, explore mentorship, or invest in a life coach. Your support team will give you objective and invaluable advice when you need it.

Use Your Imagination and get Creative

It is very natural to conjure up ideas about all sorts of things, all day long. And all day long, your mind systematically processes on average 70,000 thoughts per day. I invite you to consider using one of those thoughts as an opportunity to think about what passionate living means to you? Maybe it means flying jet planes in Thailand, or running multiple businesses worldwide. Maybe it means helping the orphans in Africa, or working with researchers in the Cure Cancer societies.

Or maybe it means spending every weekend with your best friends and family. Remember when you were younger? And the ideas seemed to run rampant? Remember when you were free? Well, the truth is, you are still just as free now as you were then, but the way you thought about things changed. Being creative is a natural gift that everyone possesses, it is just a matter of tapping back into the intuitive creativity. Use your imagination!

Actively Remove the "Dream Squashers" in Your Life

All passionate people surround themselves with other passionate, uplifting people. They choose to hang out with people who either support or facilitate their very being, and act as a complimentary addition to their lives. A "Dream Squasher" is someone who has nothing better to do but rain on everyone's parade. They are quick to judge, quick to say no, and quick to take advantage. Exactly the kind of people who ruin the very thought you may have of pursuing your passion, and creating your dreams. Even if you try, it is human nature to assimilate the environment you are in, so a powerful tip to living your passionate life is to actively remove the "Dream Squashers."

Make The Things You Love An Official Priority

Take a moment right now to list your top three (3), all-time favorite things to do. Write them down in less than a minute. I challenge you to do this right now. The first 3 things to came to your mind upon answering to this challenge are very likely a genuine list of the things you love to do.

With these 3 activities in mind, purposefully schedule in these activities as often as you can in your calendar (Google Calendar, your agenda, your iPhone or Blackberry, etc) right now. Amazingly, people tend to do the things that they write down, and tend to forget about things that are just passing thoughts. Successful and passionate people not only choose to do the things they love, they actually schedule it in. Make it an official priority!

Avoid Things that Make You Say, "Yuck!"

Have you ever been around someone that you absolutely felt "turned off" by? Have you ever participated in an activity and just felt completely repulsed by it? Have you ever said yes to something, when you deep down you just wanted to say no? All of these emotional and psychological triggers have significance in deciding where to spend your time. Passionate people choose wisely, and say yes to the things that feel good, and feel right for them. If it makes you say (think or feel) "Yuck!" then start making the daily habit of avoiding these things all together.

Get A Coach

All passionate and purposeful people have ways to track and measure their personal success. Success just means you have achieved objectives or goals you made in advance. You decide what success means to you, and in this case, the successful state is actually living more passionately and literally being in love with your life.

Successful people also ensure they keep themselves accountable to what they say they will do. All talk and no action make for a very phony life, so it is always wise to get a coach. If you have the available funds to invest in yourself, there are many professionals available and ready to come to your aid.

If you don't have the funds immediately, there are always cost-effective options such as "hiring" a very reliable friend who is already doing some of the things you wish to accomplish. A qualified amateur would be someone who is at least doing all of the things you want to do successfully and consistently. Stay accountable to your desire of living passionately and get a coach.

Lighten Up

All passionate people only focus on that which brings them joy and brings them closer to their truest, most authentic selves. So having too much on their plate (literally and figuratively) is not an option in living life to the fullest. We hear the old adage, "Less is More" and as most experts will tell you, there is much truth to this statement. Is there something that you can let go of, that is simply wasting your time and energy? Do you also have some body issues whereby you are holding on too much excess weight?

Now is the time to actively participate in removing the things in your life, and in your body, that are weighing you down. This way, you will be that much better equipped to fully enjoy your daily activities and feel the energetic benefits of living life with passion. For the love of yourself and your life, Lighten up!

Make an official decision

No ifs, ands or buts, you are going to do it! This is the exact kind of mental attitude a passionate person has about their decisions in life. Procrastination kills the energy in just about any good intention, and what's more, indecision literally puts a halt to all good things. Decide now, once and for all, that you will live passionately and on purpose. All great action, all great experience, came from a great decision. Decide, and don't look back!

Debunking Common Myths

There are several misconceptions around "following your passion" that may be hindering your success. By exposing these seven myths, it may give you the insight, inspiration, and real-world guidance you need to choose your next steps for your passion project.

You hear it all the time: "Follow your passion!" "Follow your heart!" or "Follow your dreams!" But what exactly do those catchy phrases actually mean and, more specifically, what do they not mean?

There are several common assumptions I have encountered about "following your passions." Some are completely romanticized ideas and others play on the fear, limitation, and scarcity mindset, but the assumptions in either category are indeed myths.

Here are the most common myths about "following your passions."

Pursuing Work You Are Passionate about Is Selfish and Egoistic

Many of my clients express feelings of guilt about pursuing work that has more meaning to them or that uses their passions. They have voiced fears that their dreams of finding more rewarding work are ego-driven. A common theme that emerges is, "Why should I be able to do ... ? or "Who am I to ... ?" Well, I say "Who are you to not?"

There is a common fear that spending time focusing on your passions is greedy and selfish to others, when in fact the opposite is true.

Studies have shown that pursuing and engaging in activity that you are passionate about increases happiness and well-being. In fact, a study published in the Journal of

Happiness Studies suggests that having two "harmonious passions" is even more beneficial than just one!

And the benefits don't stop at you: when a person is fulfilled and happy, it is actually beneficial to the people around them as well. In a study conducted by Harvard researchers, they found that when a person becomes happy, a friend living close by has a 25 percent higher chance of becoming happy themselves. A spouse experiences an 8 percent chance of being happy themselves and for next-door neighbors, it's 34 percent.

So not only can following your passions make you happy, it can also potentially make others happy too!

Passion Is All It Takes to Create Success or "Do What You Love, and the Money Will Follow"

Building a successful career or business by following your passion does not guarantee success or wealth, even if you are great at what you do. It does not mean you have the skills or knowledge you need to bring that passion to your market.

As Michael Gerber points out so well in his book, The E-Myth Revisited, there's a fatal assumption that so many would-be entrepreneurs make, and it's this: "If you understand the technical work of a business, you understand a business that does that technical work." The truth is quite the opposite—the technical work of a business and the business that does that technical work are two totally different things.

My advice is always to make sure you have a plan to bring your passion project to life. You should not only assess the various skills you will need to pursue your passion path, but also gain specificity about your niche and target market, and work directly with someone who has the knowledge or skills to support your endeavors.

Being highly passionate and great at what you do is an asset, but it simply does not guarantee your success.

Doing Work You Love

William MacAskill, cofounder of 80,000 Hours, a non-profit focused on helping people to find satisfying careers in which they will have the largest social impact, interviewed hundreds of people across a wide range of careers. He found that trying to pursue some preordained "passion" is the wrong way to find a career you enjoy that makes a big difference to the world.

Why? Well for starters, most people's passions just don't fit well into the world of work. The better option is to find work that feels engaging and can eventually grow into a passion.

Sometimes a passion grows from your engagement and mastery, but just as a love can grow deeper and more complex with time, so can your passion for any activity in which you are deeply engaged with.

One Day You Will Arrive at Your Passion

I have spent countless hours with clients who are trying to figure out what passion they want to pursue, assuming that once they find that passion the work will be done. The real truth is that following your passion is a journey and there is no real destination. The passion path is one that unfolds each day with a new you and a new world. Following your passion has no set path, no curriculum, and no structure; don't expect to get anywhere you will stay for too long!

You Will Never Doubt Your Direction

Deciding to pursue a passion should include a well-thought-out plan, but just because you make a plan and decide to engage in your passion doesn't mean you will be free from doubt and fear. In fact, taking risks increases uncertainty and gives doubt and fear more of an opportunity to arise. Author Seth Godin says, "Art is the act of doing work that matters while dancing with the voice in your head that screams for you to stop."

Know that it's totally normal to experience moments of doubt as you follow your passion. Create a practice that helps you deal with this. Find a support group, hire a coach, or commit to a daily meditation practice.

You Won't Make Any Money

Converse to the belief that if you follow your passion, the money will always naturally follow is the limited belief you will never make money doing something you love. There is a ton of people out there busting this myth each day! That is a reality. Rest assured, you can make millions of dollars doing something you are passionate about if that is what you choose to do. But remember, abundance and wealth have much deeper meaning than just making money. True wealth comes from deep relationships, time freedom, love, adventure, and contribution, which are all possible with a determined, focused, and realistic view of what following your passions is all about.

Leverage The Law of Attraction

Have you ever tried to turn gravity on or off? Probably not because you realize it can't be done. Well, there's another powerful force in the Universe that—just like gravity—surrounds us and affects us. It's called The Law of Attraction, and maybe we can't turn it on or off, but we can harness its tremendous benefits.

To be successful, you must learn how to use The Law of Attraction to create the life you really want. If you're already working on implementing the principles in your life, think of this as a fresh opportunity to brush up on your skills and check your progress. It takes time and consistent effort to train ourselves to behave, think, and speak in only positive ways, but the Universe rewards us exponentially with abundance, joy, and unlimited benefits. Basically, we reap what we sow, and we can freely choose to sow seeds of positivity!

Positive Action and Emotion Attract Positive Outcome

Basic chemistry tells us that a physical object, such as a house or a dog or this book, is made up of billions of individual atoms—tiny parcels of energy—that bond together into different forms such as water, metal, and plastic. Similarly, our thoughts are also a form of energy—easily detected as brain waves by standard medical equipment—that can interact with our physical world just like any other form of energy does. When we understand this basic science, we realize our thoughts can actually interact with the physical world and help bring about what we want to happen.

The core tenet of The Law of Attraction says: What you think about, talk about, believe strongly about, and feel intensely about, you will bring about. Once you know that, by using your thoughts, you can help bring about the opportunities, resources, and people who can help you accomplish your goals, you'll start paying greater attention to the direction of your thoughts and what you focus on throughout the day.

Aware of the Power of Positive Thinking

Everything—including you—is vibrating at a specific and unique frequency. That means you can learn to use the power of deliberate thought to stay in a state of higher vibration and attract what you want in life. Here's how:

Ask for what you want

Decide what you really want and use words that focus on that goal. Replace negative images and thoughts with positive ones. Consistently ask for what you want and then let the Universe worry about how you'll get it.

Believe you'll get what you want, then take action

Believing means being confident that you've put your future in the hands of a greater power and that your goals can be accomplished. Taking action is another form of belief—after all, we would only take action on goals we believe are possible to begin with.

Receive what you want

One of the best ways to bring yourself into vibrational alignment with what you want is to use affirmations—statements of your goals and desires already achieved in present time. Repeat them regularly so your subconscious mind maintains a vibrational match to what you want.

Success is not only an attitude and belief system, it's also a science. Experts on the science of success know that the brain is a goal-seeking organism, and when you give it a specific goal, it will work overtime to achieve it.

It may surprise you to also learn that the small percentage of Americans who write down their goals and regularly review them earn nine times more over the course of their lifetimes than those who don't.1 This alone should motivate you to write down your goals!

Clear about what your Goals are

If you have no criteria for measuring the successful completion of a goal, you don't have a true goal—you simply have a good idea. An actual goal that inspires action and unleashes the power of your subconscious mind must include how much (a measurable quantity) and by when (a specific time and date for completion).

One of the best ways to get clarity on your goals is to write them out in detail. When you write it all down, your subconscious will know specifically what to work on, including which opportunities to focus on to bring about success. Reread your goals three times a day—close your eyes and picture each one as if it were already accomplished and imagine how it feels to actually be living with that achievement.

Most of our goals represent incremental improvements in our life—get new car insurance, clean that closet, finish this week's sales presentation. But, what if you could work toward accomplishing a breakthrough goal—something that substantially improves life as you know it, such as buying your first home or starting a business or funding your retirement?

Those are the kind of goals that are worth pursuing with passion. Write down a few breakthrough goals for your vision—including a completion date. Then focus on those quantum leaps that will change your life.

Visualizing your Breakthrough Goal

Once a goal is set, three things will emerge that stop most people—but they're not going to stop you! They are considerations, fears, and roadblocks.

Let's say you decide to double your income by the end of the year. Before you know it, thoughts will emerge like I won't have time for my family or I'll have to work twice as many hours. These thoughts are considerations. They've been in your subconscious a long time, but now that they have come to light, you can address them and move on.

Fears, on the other hand, are feelings: You may have a fear of rejection, a fear of being laughed at, or a fear of failure. But fears are also just part of the process of moving toward your goals. Knowing that in advance helps you overcome them.

Roadblocks are purely external circumstances that an be overcome such as not having the money to start a new business or needing additional training before seeking a promotion. Roadblocks are obstacles that appear in your path, but they also are just things you will have to deal with.

Once you know to expect considerations, fears, and roadblocks, you'll realize they're not as overwhelming as you thought. Learn to accept and confront them because, more often than not, they are the very things that have been holding you back in life.

Setting a Manageable Goal

T he secret of getting ahead is getting started. The secret of getting started is breaking your complex, overwhelming tasks into small, manageable tasks, and then starting on the first one.

When you break down large goals into small tasks and accomplish them one at a time, you'll move forward much more easily. It's known as "chunking it down." That's how big goals are achieved.

One great way to discover the individual steps is to ask people who have already accomplished what you want to do. From personal experience, they can guide you through the necessary steps and give you advice on how to avoid common pitfalls. You can also purchase books or guides, take online courses, or even start from your end goal and look backward.

Imagine that you have already achieved your goal, what did you do to get where you are now? What was the last thing you did? And the thing before that? When you find the first thing you did, that's your starting point.

Asking for Guidance and Advice

Mind mapping is a simple yet powerful process for creating a to-do list for achieving your goal. It lets you determine things like who you need to talk to, what information you need to pull together, what the deadlines are that you need to meet, and more. If you've always dreamed of becoming an author and want to write your first book—a breakthrough goal that would lead to an extraordinary new career—you could use mind mapping to help you "chunk down" your very large goal into smaller steps.

Here's how mind mapping works:

1. Draw a circle in the center of a page. Inside the circle, jot down the name of your major goal (write a book).

2. Divide your goal into the major subcategories of tasks you'll need to do to accomplish the primary goal and draw a mini-circle for each (interview experts, find an agent).

3. Draw several lines radiating outward from each mini-circle and label each line with its corresponding small task (write an email asking for an interview, hire a transcriber on Fiverr.com).

4. Break down each one of the small tasks with action items to create a master to-do list.

Using Mind-Mapping Skills To Break Down Large Goals

Once you've created a mind map for your goal, you'll have to transform all of your to-do items into action items. List each item on your daily to-do list separately, along with a completion date. Transfer them to your calendar and schedule them in the proper order, then do whatever is necessary to stay on track.

We recommend you plan your day the night before—make a fresh to-do list based on the current day's accomplishments and outcomes. Spend a few minutes visualizing exactly how you want the day to go, and your subconscious mind will work during the night thinking of creative ways to reach the goals you set out to achieve.

Each morning, your plan should be to complete the most important items on your to-do list first. Here's a tip for making this a success: As soon as you take out your list, identify five things you absolutely must accomplish that day, then number them one through five, with one being the item you least enjoy and five being the item you most enjoy.

By putting the item you least enjoy at the top of your list, it becomes your first task of the day. Now, not only won't you spend the whole day thinking about it, but getting it done first creates momentum and builds confidence, setting the tone for the rest of the day.

Act As If

*"**B**elieve and act as if it were impossible to fail."*
      —Charles F. Kettering

One of the greatest strategies for success is to act as if you are already where you want to be. That requires you to think, talk, act, dress, and feel like you have already achieved your goals. Acting "as if" projects to the world a sense of confidence and achievement, sending powerful messages to your subconscious mind, which is designed to find unique ways to solve problems.

It also programs your brain's reticular activating system—the function that allows into your awareness useful information from the millions of pieces of information you process every day—to make you aware of hidden resources that may help you. What's more, when you act as if, The Law of Attraction comes into play, since acting "as if" sends strong vibrations to the Universe that you are committed to achieving your goal—and that you are open to accepting and applying anything it sends your way.

Believing and acting as if I am already where I want to be.

You can begin right now to act as if you've already achieved the goals you set for yourself. Once you start acting successful, that outer experience will create the inner experience—the feelings, emotions, confidence, and thoughts—that will lead you to the fulfillment of your goal.

How would you act if you were already a straight-A student, a bestselling author, an Olympic athlete, a top salesperson, a celebrated musician, or a successful entrepreneur? How would you think, talk, carry yourself, dress, treat other people, handle money, and so forth?

There are a couple of very important lessons we can learn from the behavior of successful people: they exude self-confidence, they've learned the power of asking for what they want, they speak up about what they don't want, they take risks and celebrate their successes, and they also save a portion of their income and share a portion with others.

These are all things that you can start to do right now. They don't cost more money, but they do require intention. And as soon as you start acting "as if," the people and things that will help you achieve your goals in real life will start being drawn to you.

Exuding Self-Confidence And Asking For What I Want With Complete Faith

It's imperative that you start now being who you want to be—don't let any more time pass while you're "thinking it over." Why? Because inaction is the same as never taking action. Start now and be who you want to be, then do the things that go along with being that person, and soon you'll find that you easily have everything you want in life—health, wealth, fulfilling relationships, and social impact.

Tania Kotsos, author and creator of Mind Your Reality, says: "It is your subconscious mind that is the storehouse of your deep-seated beliefs and programs. To change your circumstances and attract to yourself that which you choose, you must learn to program and reprogram your subconscious mind."

For thousands of years this principle has been with us and yet so few people actually put it to use. Let those words inspire you into action!

I am laying down powerful blueprints in my subconscious mind to make my dreams come true.

Take Action, Even if You Don't Know the Whole Path

*"T**hings may come to those who wait, but only the things left by those who hustle."*
—Abraham Lincoln

It's long been known by successful people that the world doesn't reward you for what you know. It rewards you for what you do. Yet, as obvious and practical as that statement is, millions of people every day get tied up analyzing, planning, and organizing instead of simply taking action. They seem to look the other way hoping the rules will change while they're preoccupied.

In the end, however, what we know or what we believe is of little consequence. The only thing that matters is what you do.

What happens the day you decide to take action? People will wake up and start paying attention to you. People with similar goals will fall into alignment with you. You will begin learning things from experience. Things that once seemed confusing will become clear, and things that once appeared difficult will become easier. You will attract others who will support and encourage you, and wonderful things will begin to flow toward you—once you take action.

Attracting People Who Are Encouraging And Supporting Me.

There's an exercise that I use in my seminars to demonstrate the power of taking action. I hold up a $100 bill and ask, "Who would like this $100 bill?" Lots of people start waving their hands back and forth. Other people shout out, "I want it!" or "Give it to me!"

But I just continue standing there holding up the $100 bill until someone actually gets out of their chair and comes up and takes it out of my hand. When I ask the group how many of them thought about standing up and coming up to take the money but stopped themselves, half the room raises their hands. What did they say to themselves?

"I was sitting too far back in the room."

"I didn't want it to look like I needed it that badly."

"I wasn't sure if you would really give it to me."

"I didn't want to look greedy."

"I was afraid I would be doing something wrong and that people would judge me or laugh at me."

"I was waiting for further instructions."

So, what did the person who actually got the money do that no one else in the room did to end up $100 richer? She got off her butt and took action—she did what was necessary to get the money—and that's exactly what you need to do if you want to be successful!

Learning from each experience When I make Mistakes.

In order to be successful, you have to do what successful people do, and successful people are highly action-oriented. If you hold yourself back for fear of looking foolish in one situation, you probably hold yourself back for fear of looking foolish in others. You have to identify those patterns, break through them, and stop holding yourself back.

Most people don't take action because they are afraid of failing. Successful people, on the other hand, realize that failure is an inevitable and natural part of the learning process. They know failure is just a way that we learn by trial and error.

Once you embrace failure as part of the journey to success, you'll be much more willing to just get started, make mistakes along the way, pay attention to the feedback you receive, make the necessary corrections, and keep moving forward toward your goal. Every experience you have will yield more useful information that you can apply to the next action you take.

So, by now, you have gone through the necessary foundational steps to success—created a vision, set specific and measurable goals, broken them down into small steps, visualized and affirmed your success, and chosen to believe in yourself and your dreams. Now it's time to take action.

How to Happy in Life and Business

There are many successful people who live their lives as they wish. They love what they do and work hard at it. You can see that the most successful ones have jobs that they love. There are many reasons for this, but one of the most important reasons is that if you are passionate about your work, you work harder because you enjoy doing it so much. So you see why this is very important, once you find your passion the easier things will be in your life.

If you don't wake up every day excited about how you make a living, then it is time to find something that truly excites you. If you are bored and unhappy with your life or what you do in your life now, then it is time for a change. You might think there are obstacles in your way, which you may be afraid to take the opportunity to change in order to make your life better. No time like now to change those things in your life you are not satisfied with and find your passion.

You have more control over your life than you might think or might have been told. Think about the things that make you happy, whether it be with money, relationships, career, etc. and then find a way to achieve that goal to live your life with passion. If you can imagine doing it, then find a way to make it happen. Nothing is beyond your reach! Now is the time to set your goals!

The amount of money you make is not really a way to measure true success. There are many people with money that are not satisfied with their lives. For those of you who will be really happy, you should follow your passions and then wealth, success and real happiness will come to you. But how do you find what you're really passionate about?

There are many ways to search and find your passions. One way to find what you like is by asking yourself about the things you enjoy. You can get ideas from things that exist in your home or something you enjoy talking about. Live your life with the passion you deserve, it is one of the reasons we're here – to enjoy life fully! You have the same capacity as everyone else and you deserve to have the passion in your life!

ENTREPRENEURS: START YOUR JOURNEY WITH PASSION!

Have you ever found an amazing business and wondered how it became so successful? It all started with two things – an entrepreneur and a passion. That may sound simple, but the truth is, a successful online entrepreneur needs passion in order to even begin their journey. Without passion, it would be the same as trying to create a business without an idea. You need passion first.

Passion Or Idea

Passion and ideas go hand in hand. However, when it comes to starting a business, an idea doesn't mean much if there isn't any passion behind it. Think about the last big idea you had. How did it make you feel? Were you excited? Energized? Ready to take on the world? You couldn't wait to get started. Now, think about chores you'd rather never have to do again. You know they have to get done, but you're not very passionate about them. In the end, you put them off for as long as possible. The big idea, the idea with passion behind it, on the other hand, took priority over everything.

Passion is what takes an idea from thought to action and on to success. The more passion behind the idea, the higher your chance for success.

Finding The Idea

Passion is great, but what if there's no idea, or substance to go with it? Once again, entrepreneur passion is here to save the day. If you want to start your own business, but aren't sure what your best options are, look no further than your current passions. Make a list of the things you are interested in or have always wanted to delve in to. Take the time to organize your list from most to least passionate. Once you have your list ready, make a second list of your strongest skills. These can be anything, not just education or job training.

Which passions do your skills match up with best? Are there one or two interests which stand out from the rest? Do you feel more excited when you consider one interest over another? Answer these questions and you've found the best passion for your business. Now it's time to find the idea.

Remember, you don't have to reinvent the wheel. Just because someone else may already have a similar business, it doesn't mean you can't start your own. Consider how many computer manufacturers there are. For the most part, each has its own unique qualities, even though the final products are fairly similar. Remember, with your personal stamp, your idea is always unique. Think carefully about what you can and want to provide your customers. Look at similar businesses, if applicable, and think about how you can tweak and improve.

Embrace Your Passion

Becoming an entrepreneur is the best time to embrace your passion. It is the starting point for every single successful entrepreneur. Let your passion guide you. It will create a slew of ideas, keep you motivated and most importantly, lead you to the success you've always dreamed of. Passion is what separates a job from a career. Use your passion to create a career of your very own, with your business at the heart.

Finding Passion In Lovemaking

Passion is a deep desire and longing, a strong desire for and enthusiasm surrounding something or someone. Being passionate includes this sense and feeling of being ruled by an all-consuming urge to engage intensely in an activity be it physical, mental or emotional. This discussion will not include passions for such things as art, music, any career or political view; instead we are focusing on utilizing your ability to understand and create passion in your sexual relationship. Where there is passion, most often there is also love.

If you are married you will need to be more creative about when, where, how long you will be intimate. Never stop being friends and lovers, that's the first key. Next, know yourself, your inner most desires and do not be afraid to bring fantasies into your sex life – with the approval of your partner of course.

You must first understand yourself and why you have gotten yourself into a boring sexual place. In counseling so many couples over the years I have been told that children tend to put a damper on relationships. I think that's a copout! Don't let the creativity die for heaven's sake! You've seen that program "Are you smarter than a fifth grader" right?

Well, put your two heads together and come up with ways to work around children. That's your job, mine here is to teach you how to become the passionate lover you desire to be, and to receive passionate advances and act upon them as well. Passion begins in the mind, but it connects every cell and directs physical and emotional reactions where there is love and enthusiasm.

Identifying passion

Just Imagine this scene. Your lover is a distance away but you can't stop thinking of her throughout the day. You connect in ways you might not even understand, there is a mingling of souls as they say and a deepness to your love.

Your drive home seems too long but your mind and body are already with her, remembering past lovemaking events. The way she walks, her smile, her intellect, her spontanaeity, and sensitive ways; and oh her soft skin, great body, the way she responds to you and how she makes you feel sensual. She calls you and says something naughty and you can't wait to get home.

It's been a long day at the office, and you had an exhausting dinner meeting. You come home, your favorite music is playing, the fragrance of candles is in the air, the fireplace is on and your lover greets you at the door. She puts her arms around you wearing your favorite perfume, her hair is a little different showing her neck, and she kisses your lips, it's a warm wet kiss. She is wearing something very seductive, but not too much skin yet showing. She takes your briefcase as you slip off your shoes. She walks upstairs with you and helps you remove your coat, tie, and pants. You freshen up as she tells you she will be downstairs waiting for you. This is different, pleasing and exciting as well.

You come down the stairs and she has removed an article of clothing that creates a reaction. She takes your hand and brings it close to her body allowing a gentle caress but nothing more. She has arranged a comfortable place with a blanket and pillows on the living room floor in front of the fireplace. She hands you your favorite drink.

You haven't made love there before. You start to talk but she touches her finger to your lips as if to say shhh, I understand you. She begins to kiss your hand, seductively sucking one of your fingers and your imagination runs wild. Emotions within you stir and impulses are strong. She dips her hands in warm massage oil as you relax comfortably on the pillows. It feels as if she is reaching inside of you somehow and your body begins involuntary movements.

This is all about you now, as you close your eyes for a moment wanting this to last. She pulls away and blows gently on the oiled spots. You can hardly stand it as she continues to bring her body closer to you allowing parts of her body to brush against you.

She is also aroused and as desirous as you are, but with restraint you both allow the passion to rise while you explore new erogenous zones watching and listening for just the right reaction. It is evident she wants to please you and you want to please her as well; it is not just a physical pleasure that you both seek, but a spiritual one as well.

You feed each other cooled berries dipped in your favorite alcohol and the juice runs down your skin and hers as well. Deep desire and emotions rise as never before...there is a newness, almost as if a different person is making love to you, while at the same time, you love the deep connection beyond the physical even now. You haven't wanted each other so much in a long while... and then the deepest passionate connection.

That's a sense of a passionate scene. What was happening internally? What makes you desire someone so much that all other thoughts disappear? Lust is not passion. So if you do not know your lover very well, and you are not in love with one another, sharing passion is not what you will experience. Being sexually stimulated by someone without love certainly happens all of the time.

This discussion surrounds identifying with passion to the core of your being, that which some have described as champagne running through their veins. Passion does not necessarily create a sexual reaction, but it does elicit a fire in the heart, a yearning so unlike simple sex that you are blown away by the experience.

Next, what will make you more desirable? What will create the automatic wave of passionate desire for you in your partner?

In order to find your passion you must discover yourself and then understand and make discoveries about your partner. Passionate love making does not just call for intensity, it calls for love. An individual can be an artful lover, but not passionate. Zealousness does not always equate to passion. There is a chemistry that unites two lovers on levels that move beyond the physical.

If love is definable, and I don't know if it is truly possible to define love with human words; than passion is definitely one of the components in that equation. We must desire someone so much that the core of our being is rocked by the site of them, by their touch, by their words, by the thought of them.

One must be able to elicit a reaction at a distance for passion to exist. Fantasies definitely come into the picture of passion as imagery is powerful. So before you see your lover you must begin imagining them. Imagine what it will feel like to hold them, to touch them, to kiss them, and to be intimate. Make them part of your fantasy before it happens.

If your love life has gone stale and you want to change things dramatically, take a look at the suggestions below:

Identify your own sexual thirst and pleasures. First each of you should write down everything you can think of that turns you on and that you find erotic. Think about any fantasies you have had or anything sexual you've wanted to try or thought was interesting. Try to make as thorough a list as possible and get creative. If you don't have any ideas rent some movies if need be.

Next write down what you think your partner most enjoys and be specific. Understanding your partner on all levels will help you create passionate love making. If you know your partner enjoys silk sheets, a warm bath, roses, a massage, walking on the beach, listening to Beethoven or Bach, dancing, hot movies, then make these things part of the experience. Make changes as your moods and interests change... be flexible.

Discuss your lists. Does he or she find the items erotic? Would he or she be interested in trying one or more? Sense their reactions on every level. Look into his or her eyes and determine if they are unable to say the words you need to hear. Talk about how you would try the items or if you or your partner wanted any variation or would need to negotiate any boundaries or limits of what would be tried. Through examining these lists, you may learn something new about your partner.

Decide which items you both find erotic and interesting. Have one partner plan a time for you to be together and sexual. Surprise each other and for heaven's sake be spontaneous occasionally. Lovemaking is quite boring when you have to schedule it into your day or night. Shower together...that can be really fun! Or take a whirlpool bath together; be sure to add fragrant candles for mood lighting, play beautiful music, and lay in one another's arms while you soak – let things happen.

It is not uncommon for couples to have different sexual desires. In fact that can make things even more fun! Passion includes enthusiasm for making each other's fantasies happen, as well as for making your own happen. Your partner will appreciate that you took an interest in something that he or she would like and it sends the signal that it is o.k. for you both to have different sexual tastes, that you are attentive to his or her needs as a sexual person, and that you receive pleasure from watching him or her get turned on.

You may find over time that you not only enjoy giving your partner pleasure, but that you enjoy the activity as well. We often don't know what we might like unless we give it a try a few times. If you are willing to be more open to your partner's ideas, it is likely that he or she will be more open to your ideas as well.

Lovemaking should begin long before any sexual act. Perhaps walking hand-in-hand along a beautiful path, or window shopping; sitting at a ball game, watching birds in the park, going for a ride and touching each other playfully while driving (be careful); do whatever it is that brings you to the playful side of life, the tender moments.

Have you really explored each other on every level? Try playing a sexual game. Go to an adult shop and pick out something together.

Make life a party whenever possible. Celebrate each other beyond the bedroom. Pleasure one another in ways that do not include physical intimacy. Learn to bend so you do not break apart.

Love what you do and do what you love more often. Stop juding your body or your partners. Love them from inside out. With age comes body changes and challenges. If you are truly in love with someone passion will remain high because you will move intimacy to "higher ground;" the mind and the spirit.

Upgrade your look from head to toe every six months. Keep things fresh and exciting. Make the space where you spend most of your lovemaking time the most glorious space possible. Make it sexy for both of you.

Creating passion is about being creative and experimenting in ways that feel comfortable, pleasurable, and exciting. Sexual expression in our relationships is about sharing love and having fun. So have fun, and allow the passion within you to create moments that are extraordinary! Once you create the moments, a lifetime of passionate love will be yours if you continue to be attentive to your needs and your lover's needs as well.

Conclusion

S o, what have we learned? To recap: Don't drop everything and charge off once you find your passion – a steady hand may allow you to enjoy it more and save you from ruin. Don't also assume your passion has to be a viable business, it may be unprofitable except as a hobby – if you think it could be a business, seek proper advice to ensure your execution is also correct.

Check too on what the fruit of your passion is – whether it leads to healthy things in your life, or unhealthy. Again, your particular expression of that passion is key here. Finally, we learned that jumping to conclusions about what your passion is may stop you from recognising several other passions you also have. Don't miss out if you don't have to!

-- Logan Hawkins

Dear Reader,

Thanks for exploring this book with me. Now that you know how to find your passion and purpose in life...

...could you kindly leave a review?

Thanks,

Logan

P.S. Reviews are like giving a warm hug to your favorite author.

We love hugs.

https://www.amazon.com/dp/B084ZWJPQF

Check Out Other Books

Mental Toughness Handbook Series

The 7-Day Self Discipline Blueprint: Get Things Done and Unleash Your Inner Drive

The 7-Day Self Discipline Blueprint: The Modern Applications of Stoicism

The 7-Day Self Discipline Blueprint: Habit Stacking for Beginners

Productivity Books Series

Find Your Max: Improve Work Productivity with Time Management Magic

Find Your Organization: Get Your Life in Order and Stay Clutter-Free

www.ingramcontent.com/pod-product-compliance
Lightning Source LLC
Chambersburg PA
CBHW020613220526
45463CB00006B/2575